My First BASEBALL SEASON

EDNA FELICIANO-FLATTS

AuthorHouse™
1663 Liberty Drive
Bloomington, IN 47403
www.authorhouse.com
Phone: 1 (800) 839-8640

Published by AuthorHouse 01/24/2017

ISBN: 978-1-5246-6882-2 (sc)
ISBN: 978-1-5246-6881-5 (e)

Library of Congress Control Number: 2017901125

Print information available on the last page.

Any people depicted in stock imagery provided by Thinkstock are models,
and such images are being used for illustrative purposes only.
Certain stock imagery © Thinkstock.

This book is printed on acid-free paper.

Because of the dynamic nature of the Internet, any web addresses or links contained in this book may have changed
since publication and may no longer be valid. The views expressed in this work are solely those of the author and do not
necessarily reflect the views of the publisher, and the publisher hereby disclaims any responsibility for them.

authorHOUSE®

First Year

The baseball season is beginning. Oh boy! I am so ready to play! But I have no clue how to play because I was in T-ball last year. During T-ball, all I did was hit the ball that the coach put on a stick. Once I hit the ball, I had to run to the bases, but instead I hopped the whole way without getting into trouble with the coach. I made everyone laugh when it was my turn to bat.

Hey, I'm only six years old, going to be seven, and I am so excited to play this year. Will it be the same as last year? I don't know. This year I've been moved up to play with the eight years old kids. My teammates are bigger than I am. Maybe I won't be able to hop or skip through the bases. I almost forgot! My dad is my coach too. Oh no! What am I to do? How can I have fun this year with my dad as a coach? Boy! I am only six years old, almost seven. I think I have too much to worry about, and the season has just begun.

Here we go! At practice, I'm the only one they call out all the time.

"Anthony, do this!"

"Anthony, do that!"

Is there going to be any fun for me this year? My dad gets mad, and sometimes he tells me he's going to put me back in T-ball. But if I go back there, everyone is going to call me a baby. And I don't want that to happen.

Well, let me tell you about this season. I'm playing for the Indians. Some of my teammates are from my school and my class. With my eyes, wide open, I realize they can make fun of me. Oh no!

Did I mention that I also play with my second-oldest brother, Eric? He's good, or so he thinks. He's been playing a bit longer than I have. He's seven, turning eight, but he can't catch too well. Shhh! We should keep it a secret. I don't want him to get mad at me too.

Now that the baseball season has begun, my dad has us practicing. We've been practicing and practicing, and let me tell you that the weather has been very cold. Hmmm! Why is it cold when it's time for our practice? I don't like to practice in the cold for an hour. My hands hurt, and my legs start shivering. And when that happens, I can't concentrate.

In some of the practices, my dad says, "Today we're going to warm up and stretch."

But why would I need to stretch? Last year all I had to do was hit the ball and skip to the base. There was no stretching.

You see—this is my dad's first year coaching, and he doesn't know how to do anything right just yet. Let me tell you a little about my dad. He loves baseball, but he'd rather play softball instead. I guess it's because the ball is bigger and softer. I don't know. I'm only six years old, almost seven.

My mom tells me all the time, "Anthony, Daddy is out of shape, and that's why he doesn't play baseball."

And I ask, "What's out of shape, Mom?"

She says, "It's when you have a hard time doing something, and when you do, you get tired fast."

Oh! Now I know why my dad just sits on the bench and yells all the time, "Run to first base when you hit the ball, Anthony."

I know it's because he's out of shape. He also has other parents helping him coach. That's my dad. He's out of shape, like my mom says.

It's time for some more practice, and I'm so excited today. My dad bought my brother and me new cleats to wear. They're going to help me run fast. But my mom says I can't wear them for practice. They're for when we play our first game. Eric is going to be a catcher, but I don't know why if he can't catch the balls thrown to him.

See, in my case, my dad doesn't know where to put me. I think he's confused because I play really well. Even though I am six, almost seven, I'm as good as Eric or Kris, my biggest brother.

When I play the outfield, I hear everyone calling my name, "Anthony! Anthony!"

And when I yell back, "What?" they all yell, "Didn't you see the ball?"

I look all around to see where the ball went, but I don't see it until I hear my dad yell, "Anthony, you need to put out the glove the right way and catch the ball."

At times when I play the outfield, the ball is hit, but it doesn't reach where my dad tells me to stand. I don't know I have to move from my spot to get the ball. I think the ball will reach where I'm standing.

Sometimes I can't understand why they're all yelling. I can hear them. They don't need to yell!

And if they aren't yelling, I see my dad start walking to the outfield to say, "Anthony, I'm going to tell you one more time. You need to put the glove down, and with your other hand, you scoop the ball. Then you step forward and throw it to the kid playing shortstop."

I say, "Okay, Dad. I got it."

As my dad walks away, he yells, "Bat that ball to the outfield." Then he turns and says, "Anthony, be ready. The ball is coming to you."

I scoot down and put my glove in place. I'm ready for the ball to come to me. The ball is hit so hard that it goes over my head. All I can do is look as it goes above my head toward the fence.

Then I hear my dad yell, "Go get that ball and throw it in."

I turn and start running to the fence to get the ball. I get it and throw it in to the shortstop, but he isn't ready. So, my dad again walks to the field and starts talking to the boy at shortstop. I want to show my dad that I know how to play, so I ask him to change my position to shortstop. So, my dad now switches me to shortstop. I can play shortstop with my eyes closed, and I tell him so.

He asks, "How would you do that? If you close your eyes, you won't see the ball coming your way."

I say, "I learned shortstop from Kris."

Yes, Kris plays shortstop all the time.

I love baseball, and maybe when I get older, I'd like to play for my dad's favorite team, the New York Yankees. Oh, I forgot. That's Kris's team name too, the Yankees. He's in the Minor A league. That means he's not in the majors, but he's close to it.

Let me tell you a little bit about my big brother Kris because he is extremely good. Kris started playing baseball when he was five. My mom says that Kris is still afraid of hitting the ball when it's his turn to bat because he's the shortest player in his league. I think Kris has been playing baseball for four years now, and we always watch all his games.

Trust me. He wasn't so good at first. Oh no! When he started to play, he was in the outfield. To me, it seemed like he wasn't paying attention at all. When he was playing the outfield during games, the ball never went to him. So he didn't move from his position. As he played, his coaches moved him from outfield to shortstop, and I guess they liked how he played shortstop more than the outfield.

This year, I think Kris's team is going to the championship. I always hear my mom say that she wants to go see Kris play in Williamsport. Who knows what that means? It would be funny if they put him playing outfield again. That way he doesn't have to do much work. Maybe that's why I am so good. I learned it from my big brother Kris.

Oh, he's smart too. He gets all A's in school, and he plays the violin. When Kris doesn't have practice, he helps my dad with the team. You know my dad needs a lot of help. It's his first-time coaching, and he doesn't know much.

Finally, we get our uniforms, and I love it. My uniform is the best. It's red and blue. I think I look better than Eric does, but don't tell him. I don't want him to go and cry to Mom. He always goes and cries to Mom, even when Dad yells at him for not catching the ball.

I'm really excited! Opening Day is in three more days, and we're going to have our first game. Wow! I hope I get to go first at bat. But I also want to be a pitcher, a first baseman, and shortstop. I don't know. I want to do all of them. I am going to get to wear my awesome uniform, and it looks so cool on me. I am going to hit a home run in the first inning. Oh, yes I will! But first, another practice is tomorrow.

Another day after being so tired from school, I have to get ready to go to my practice. I have to change my clothing and be on the way to the park with my dad and Eric. Yes! Like I said, it's always cold when I have practice. It's so cold that I want to go home, but my mom took my dad's car, and I have no choice but to stay here in the cold all through the practice. To top it off, we have to be in the park a half hour early so my dad can get everything done before my teammates get there. He does not want us to help him. Instead he has Eric and me do stretches. I am thinking, *Why do we have to do so much stretching if we are going to grow no matter what?*

When everyone starts arriving at the park, my dad starts talking and talking and talking. I think he's going to talk all through the practice. See, I guess it's because my mom doesn't listen to him and we have no choice. Once he's done talking, he gives us the lineup for practice, but before starting, he has us run around the baseball field two times. We all run. Once we finish, we sit in the cold bench in the dugout and wait to see what he has planned for today.

I get really excited because my dad says, "Anthony, you're going to be shortstop today."

I feel like Derek Jeter, and I love Derek Jeter! He's my favorite player, along with my mom's and Kris's too. I know that today I am going to do well.

Eric does very well today. He finally gets to catch three balls as a catcher. All through the practice, my dad tells us that we are going to bat up, and I get so happy because I want to bat first. But instead my dad has me waiting and waiting. I get so bored of waiting to bat that I start playing with my teammates in the dugout. I wait so long that I think he isn't going to let me bat.

Everyone is batting, and I am asking, "Is it my turn yet? Let me bat now!"

But he never calls me up to bat. Again, I wait and wait until almost the end of practice.

As I am standing there, all of a sudden, my dad says, "Anthony, you're up to bat."

As I step up to the batting box, it hits me. I no longer have the stick holding the ball, like I did in T-ball. I start getting scared of the ball hitting me because the boy who went before me got hit with the ball. Oh boy! Was he crying!

Not me. I just decide that I'm not going to hit the ball. I just move back and let the ball go by. Then my dad and his helper start telling me to hit the ball. I look at my dad. Boy, he doesn't seem too happy. I guess he's cold and wants to go home. So, I have no choice but to swing my bat and hit the ball. I start swinging my bat to hit the ball.

Let me tell you. My dad starts saying, "Anthony, hit the ball already. Concentrate, and swing that bat when you see the ball coming toward you."

I look at my dad and think, *Can't he see that's what I'm doing?* But he doesn't know much about baseball, so I say, "Okay, Dad."

I guess I'm not making him too happy because he starts yelling, "Get ready! He's running after this pitch."

I hit the ball, and I run to first and second. And while my dad isn't looking, I skip to third, but because Eric and I are the last kids to bat, he tells me to keep running to home base. Yes! I hit the ball finally. I am so happy.

Now it's Eric's turn. Let's see if he can hit the ball like me. Eric is in the batter's box! I can tell he's so excited. I am playing third base, and I can see it on his face. Boy! It takes him five pitches before until he finally hits the ball. I guess I did better than Eric did! Shhh! Don't say anything. You know he gets mad quickly, and besides, today is his birthday.

Practice is over. My dad gets us all together, along with the parents, and starts to talk about the thing that are going to happen before Opening day.

He says, "Parents, on March 20 at eight in the morning, be here at the park for the parents' workshop. Everyone is required to help out."

The faces on all the parents there, especially the mothers, seem like they got upset once my dad said that. They say, "Yeah, right! You'll be here by yourself, Coach!"

Once he does his talk, he also mentions that Opening Day is April 3, but we aren't going to play on that day. That makes me a little mad because I have been practicing all this time for Opening Day. He also mentions that everyone needs to be at the park at eight thirty in the morning because we need to take our team pictures. The parade will follow.

Opening Day

Opening Day is here! Mom wakes us up at seven thirty in the morning to get dressed and finally wear our cool Indians uniforms with our new cleats. Kris is wearing his Yankees uniform, but I think our Indians uniforms look better.

It's now eight o'clock, and we are on our way to the park to take our team pictures. As we arrive at the park, it's cold outside, and we get our stuff out of the car. Mom and Dad grab our baseball bags and take out our new bats. They tell us to go sit with the rest of our teammates. As we sit there, all we do is wait and wait. I get so cold that I want to go home, but I can't. Mom gets us hot chocolate, but it gets so cold that I don't want to wait anymore.

Since it isn't our turn yet to take our team pictures, I start playing and jumping around with my teammates. We start running around, and the next thing you see, all of the kids at the park start doing the same.

Since everyone at the park is running around and not ready for pictures, my dad gets mad and says, "Everyone come and take a seat here on the bench."

He doesn't understand that we are cold! We all come gather and stand on the bench, sitting for just a little because it's really cold. It's so cold that my mom goes to the car and sits there with the heater on. And when you look around, everyone is bundled up. Not even my dad can stand the cold. He's hopping in place too.

It's our turn to take the pictures, and boy, we all look so cool. After we take our pictures, we still have to wait for Kris and his team to take their pictures before we can go home.

Unfortunately, once pictures are done, we have to be back to the park at 11:40 a.m. to be prepared for the parade.

It's eleven thirty, and here we are, back at the park for the parade. Let me tell you—the parade is boring. Everyone from CLL League arrives to the park, and all of the players from every team is there. They are wearing their uniforms, but I look nice in mine!

Anyhow, we start lining up behind the school in the school playground. But not me! I go to the playground. The weather has warmed up a little bit since the morning. It's time that we go to the park. I want to run around and play tag until I think I hear my dad yell my name. I get scared and look to see where he is, but he isn't there. So, I go back to play, and I hear my name again.

This time, one of the other coaches is calling for me. My dad forgot his camcorder, so he had to go back home to get it. I don't know where my mom went to either. I guess they both went home.

As I go to Coach Jim, he says, "Anthony, you need to stay here because we are about to line up to start the parade."

I look up and say, "Okay, Mr. Jim."

I am in line, but I start to play rock-paper-scissors. Shoot, I don't even know my parents came back. Yikes!

It's time for the president of the league to make his speech and name all the teams and their coaches. At this time, we all line up with our teams. Every team from T-ball to the big kids team line up. The president announces the teams and wishes us well on our baseball season. We do the "Star-Spangled Banner" and the Little League pledge. Then three drummers from the middle school band start to sound their drums. Two kids are holding the American flag and the CLL League flag. As the drum rolls, it starts the kids with the flag lined up behind, and we start marching.

Rum pum pum pum … Rum pum pum pum. Behind the flag boys is the president. Then the first line is T-ball teams, then Minor A teams, Minor B teams, Major A teams, Major B teams, and then the girls' softball teams. We start marching from behind the school yard, go up the block, then head around the block, and come back through the parking lot of the park. Finally, we line up in the baseball field. Yes, that's all we do! We follow the flag and the three drum boys. And we march around the block. Can't we go from behind the school and head into the park? No. Not with CLL. We have to show off and march around the block and then head back to the park.

What a parade, huh! But not my mom. She isn't going to do all that. She places the camcorder at the school yard as we line up and starts recording as we march. Once the last girls' team marches, she turns off the camcorder and walks up through the playground to the park. And she starts recording again as we start entering the park. She doesn't walk as much as we did. She's the smart one. All the other mothers walk with the parade. I wish I would have stood with my mom. It would have saved me the walk!

After the parade around the block, again the president of the league gets back on the microphone and gives a speech. As he is giving his speech, a helicopter hovers on top of the field and starts to drop baseballs onto the field. We all start yelling with excitement, but not for long. The president again starts to talk and explains the rules of the league. That speech makes me want to fall asleep. Even my dad looks like he is about to drift off too.

During the speeches, a parent is going around selling raffle tickets, so after the speech, one of the parents goes to the pitcher's mound and yells out a number.

They say, "The winning raffle ticket number is six eight nine three seven."

Then we hear a lady yell, "That's my number! I got it!"

The lady gets her winnings, and now they start welcoming the new coaches to the league and awarding the veteran, whatever that is. But this is like I said, boring! We are falling asleep. I look at my dad, and I see he can't even keep his eyes open.

I start telling my friend, "Look at my dad."

We giggle because he's falling as sleep.

After they call out the awards and do all those boring speeches, they yell out, "The season has officially started! Let's play ball."

As excited as I am, I know we aren't going to play today. We have to watch Kris again. Yay! He gets lucky. His first game is today. But not us. We have to wait.

The Games

It's another week, and we don't have a game. For that reason, we have to watch Kris play his game. My mom and dad watch the game while Eric and I go to the playground. I like to watch his games, but I'd rather play on the playground with the other kids and have fun.

As we are in the park, I see my dad jump out his chair and start yelling, "Yes, we got this. Let's go, Yankees! Three up! Three down!"

I walk toward the baseball field, and I see they have two outs. The guy batting has two strikes. No one is on base yet. Now I know why my dad is excited.

The pitcher winds up. He throws, and all you see is all the parents get up from their seats.

The umpire shouts, "Strike three! You're out!"

Then you hear the parents cheer and clap.

It's time to switch now. The Yankees are batting. Here comes the first batter. The pitcher pitches the ball.

The umpire yells out, "Strike one."

In the background, you hear my mom say, "Okay, now you know. The next time he throws like that, you need to swing at it."

I ask myself, "Since when did Mom become a professional baseball announcer?"

The pitcher winds up again and throws his second pitch.

"Ball one," the umpire yells.

And again, here is my mom yelling, "Good eye, Tito!"

Here's another pitch. And click! Tito hits a line drive right through the pitcher and past the shortstop, right into left field. All I see is the excitement of all the parents. Tito runs to first base. Then the coach starts yelling and telling him to run to second base. As he's running, the kid in the outfield runs, gets the ball, and throws it to second base. The second baseman catches the ball. Tito slides to the base, and the umpire yells, "Safe!"

Everyone starts to cheer.

As the game continues, the score is thirteen to eleven. It's the bottom of the ninth inning. Bases are loaded with one out. Here comes Kris up for bat. My parents are so excited. The coaches give Kris the signs. He gets ready. The pitcher winds up, and he pitches. Kris follows his coach's direction and bunts. The ball goes in between the pitcher and the catcher. Kris starts running to first. The kid on third base runs home. He's safe! Unfortunately, Kris is out.

Here comes Jay. The Yankees now have two outs. Two kids are on base. It's up to Jay to save the game. The pitcher winds up and releases the pitch. Jay swings, and that ball is like a bird in the sky, flying all the way past the baseball field gate. It's a home run! Everyone runs to the home plate and congratulates Jay for the hit. There goes the game! Like I mentioned, Kris's team is good. The final score is seventeen to eleven. Kris can play really well.

My mom always says, "He's my little Derek Jeter."

I look at her and ask, "How about me?"

She tells me, "You're my little rascal."

I love my mom, even though I don't know what she means by "little rascal." I think my mom is a cool mom. She never misses our games. She always complains about it, but she never misses one game. She looks more excited watching our games than my dad's. I guess it's because he only plays softball.

I also think that my dad can't hit the ball. He swings and misses all the time. It is boring for us to watch my dad's team lose all the time. That's no fun. All they do is hit and pop up into the outfield. Then the outfielder catches the ball. They are always out anyway, so why play?

I like the way I play. See, I love that the crowd yells my name when it's my turn. My dad is always telling me that I need to pay more attention when I am in the field, but you see—I do. I guess he doesn't know it because this is his first-time coaching.

It's finally our first game, and it's against NE. We are the home team, so they get to bat first. (In this division, the coach pitches to us. Okay, we're not ready yet for kids pitching to us.)

Coach pitches to him, and he misses.

"Strike one!" the umpire yells.

Coach pitches again.

"Strike two!" the umpire yells.

That's right! We got them now!

Coach pitches again.

"Strike three!" the umpire yells. "You're out!"

This is going to be an easy game. I feel it coming. But they are also very long games. They take forever.

We are almost at the end of the inning, and the score is unknown. The coach won't tell us because they don't want anyone to brag.

"That stinks! What's that all about?"

Bragging is fun in baseball. My dad should know. He brags every time when he beats us in MLB on PlayStation. We don't cry about it. Yeah! By the way, that's where he learns his skills from. But that's between us, okay? He learns everything from playing the MLB game—the rules of the game, the plays, and the game—because he only plays softball in real life.

Yes, like I said, our games are super long, and everyone gets to hit. There is a lineup, but the way they have us play is that every kid bats and each kid plays the field. Once our game is complete and everyone from both team gets to play, we all line up, shake hands, and say, "Good game."

Our next game is next week, and we play LN League. They are good. I hope we can win at least once. I have to tell my dad to play his game so he can get new strategies for us. Ha ha!

Well, let me tell you. That doesn't work. I see the disappointment on my dad's face. Yup! We lose! I know we did. We barely have any good hits, and when we do, the kids don't run as fast to the bases. Eric is our backup catcher, and he also makes some mistakes. I think that we just don't play as well today as we should have. And my dad is so upset that he throws his hat on the floor with his book.

At that moment, I know we aren't winning.

My mom walks up to the dugout and tells my dad, "Honey, don't worry!" But it's with a smile because my mom always has a smile. Everything is funny to her. She makes me laugh too, even when I'm in trouble and my dad is yelling at me.

She also tells him, "Babe, Anthony tried his best out there. Give him a hug for trying because he's so little compared to the other kids."

Yeah! He puts me to play outfield, and these kids at LN League are big! They hit the ball hard too! I'm not able to get any of the balls that are hit to the outfield, but I try, like my mom said to.

Now it's close to the middle of the season, and half the time, my dad has to work. My mom says he's working overtime, whatever that means. To me, that means he's going to miss the games.

Instead of getting upset for not having my dad at the park, I take this time to have fun and feel like when I was in T-ball. When my dad is not here, I have fun because I know I won't get yelled at for anything. The other coaches are soft. They are not like my dad. He is tough and serious.

Today we are going to NE Little League park to play against them. So far they hardly ever win any of their games. We go play them at their park, and like I said, those kids are not like us. We practice so much. So, this time we are ready to show them who we are. But sometimes it gets boring because these games take so long.

We win, I guess. I see the coaches smiling, and I hear my mom calling my dad to let him know how we did. And she says, "Honey, you missed it. The boys did a great job."

I grab Eric and give him a hug. Even though it was long, I had so much fun there because the coaches didn't yell at me for hopping to base. They didn't even yell for not catching the ball that fell in front of me in the outfield. Yikes! If only my dad would have been here. He would be excited, but also he'd be yelling at me for skipping and missing the ball. But at least we did a good job, and I know he'll be happy.

Next week we are playing LL league, and my dad is missing that game too. And you know that they are undefeated? They have beaten all of our teams as well as Kris's team. His team has not won yet against LL. They are good. Even the park looks like a professional park, like the one on TV. These kids are so good, especially when they bat up. They don't miss a hit. They hit all the balls that are pitched to them, whether they hit straight to the field or foul balls to the side, where everyone needs to run out of the bleachers so they won't get hit with the ball. When we play them, we always lose, and it's because they are so good. I think I should be playing for this team. Do they need a player like me?

Well, we also need to play against NE League, but to me, they don't know how to play. It's not like LL, who are undefeated. NE League forfeited like five games because they were scared to lose against the Indians. That's my team.

So today is a great day. We don't have any practice, and Dad doesn't have to work that overtime. After doing my homework, we ask Dad if we can all play catch outside and he says yes. I am excited.

Oh, my God! My dad just hit me with the ball on my nose! Ouch! I am hurting! See what I mean? He can't throw the ball or play either. Here comes my mom, running. She is always worried about all of us.

"What did you do, Jaime?" she asks.

He says, "I pitched the ball, and it hit him in the nose."

My mom asks, "Anthony, are you okay, baby?"

I say, crying, "I think so."

My mom is worried because I am bleeding a lot. She says to my dad, "Babe, I think he needs to go to the hospital. We need to take him."

He says, "Okay, it looks like his nose is broken. Yes, it has to be broken. It's so flat."

One of my teammates also got hit with the ball at the park. I guess that today is get-hit-with-the-ball day. My teammate was worse off. He lost one of his teeth!

My mom and dad take me to the hospital. They take me to a room, and the lady says she is going to take a picture of my nose.

I ask, "Really? You can see in my nose?"

After the picture, the nurse takes me back to the room where my parents are, and we wait for the doctor to come back.

The doctor comes in and says, "It's just a small fracture."

I don't know what that means. All I know is that's it for me. I am done playing baseball. My nose hurts a lot, and it's flat. I don't want to play anymore baseball. I'd rather do boxing, flag football, or karate. I am glad the season is almost over for Eric and me, but not for Kris. His team made it to the playoffs, and now we still have to go to the park to see him play.

Bummer! That's boring sometimes. Why do they torture me this way? Well, let's end the season as winners. That way, my dad can feel good about being a first-time coach. He should feel good. It doesn't matter if we win or lose. This is Minor B. We are just learning.

During our last few games, my mom is going around, telling other mothers that she is going to get gifts for the coaches for all the hard work and dedication they did this baseball season, whatever that means. All I know is that some of the moms didn't like my dad's way of coaching. They would whisper and talk. I know because that's what my mom told my dad. Even though my mom isn't like the other moms in the park, she is a cheerleader for all of the kids. Whether we do good or bad, she always cheers. Some of the other mothers would make a circle and talk to each other on what they thought of my dad.

So, in the car on the ride home, Mom would tell Dad that some of the moms were talking about him, and so did some of the other coaches.

Dad would reply to her, "I don't care." He'd also say, "I am not part of the politics that goes on in the park, and I don't favor any kids when we are on the field, not even my own."

So, I look at them, thinking, *What's going on?* But then again, I am six turning seven, and I think this is too much for me right now.

As we get home, the last thing my mom says is, "I just hear what goes on around the field and among the parents, but not that I care. I tell you because it's not right. That's all."

As they step out the car, they kiss, and it's over just like that. I love my parents. They are the coolest.

Oh yes! My birthday is coming soon! It's on July 4. I am a Statue of Liberty baby. That's when we all celebrate Independence Day. We have played sixteen games, and we think we've won twelve of them. With all the training, we had before Opening Day, we'd better.

You know what it's like to come to the park when it's cold outside because it's always cold when we have to practice. For half of these practices, my mom took the car with her so I had no choice but to stay with my dad and practice.

That's the worst, and to think I want to do this again next year. Nope, I don't think so. I don't know about Eric. He likes to play backup catcher since Dad said he has improved on his catch. He has picked up his speed a little with all the practices, but to be honest, he still can't catch or throw. Shh! Don't say anything. We don't want him to cry to mom.

Here we are, close to the playoffs, thank God. In a few more weeks, it's over for me. No more baseball. It's swimming time!

The Final Game

Finally, the big day has arrived, my last game of the season. I am ready! I don't know about Eric. He only wants to be a catcher, but for this game, my dad says, "Someone else needs to try too."

See, Eric is scared to catch the ball. He moves away when the coach pitches the ball, and then he says, "Why do you throw that ball so fast? You want to hurt me?"

Well, that's Eric. He just can't play as good as I can! Ha! I am the best. That's why I took a hit for my team, and for that, I am able to walk to first base. Wow! The score is four to two. We have four, okay. It's the second inning, and these kids are hitting the ball. Wait a minute. Am I missing something here? The last time we played these kids, they were not doing well. I don't know what happened, but today they seem like they're playing better than before. Oh no! Now they caught up with us. It's four to four. We need to make a run. This time I'm running. I am going to run and run, not skip. We need to win!

Hey! They score two more runs, and I can't understand why. I look over to my dad, and he's already pulling his hair. If he pulls a little harder, he won't have any left by the time this game is over. It's our turn to bat, and the lineup is Sack, Gabe, Hector, Brandon, Jay, Cobe, Dylan, Eric, Ryan, Patrick, Rickie, and me. Why do I have to be last? I guess it's like my mom always says, "They save the best for last."

And I, Anthony, am the best! No one has scored yet, and Sack goes first to bat. He practices his swings. He puts one foot in the batter's box. He places the next foot. He gets his bat ready. The coach makes the first pitch, and Sack makes contact. He hits the ball. The ball passes the second baseman. Sack runs to first base, and he is safe. Here goes Gabe. He's up to bat. The coach pitches.

The umpire yells, "Ball one."

The coach pitches again, and Gabe swings the bat and misses the ball.

In the background, the umpire yells, "Strike one … Strike two … You're out."

As we go through the lineup, only Sack, Hector, and Brandon get on base. This game has me on the edge of the bench. It's Jay's turn. The coach pitches, and Jay hits the ball so hard to the outfield. Wow! He's running to first base and then second. And then he slides to third base. Cool!

Now we are all hyped and cheering. We feel the excitement in the field. We are cheering for Cobe to bat up. He swings.

"Strike one," the umpire says.

The pitcher throws the ball again.

"Ball one," the umpire says.

The coach makes another throw.

"Ball two," the umpire says.

He pitches again.

Cobe swings and misses.

The umpire yells, "Full count."

But on his next pitch, Cobe swings and gets out. Now batting is Dylan, and he hits the ball but only makes it to first base. Brandon runs home, and we score! Ah! Ah! Ah! Who's winning now?

Now it's Eric's and Ryan's turn to bat up. They both hit the ball, but the centerfielder and second baseman catch their hits. So, they are both out. In Minor A, the whole team has to bat before it's the next team's turn. So now it's Patrick's and Rickie's turn. Patrick hits and makes it to first base, and Rickie gets up. My mom is cheering. She's always cheering. He misses the first pitch. He misses the second pitch. Now he hits the ball!

My mom is yelling, "Go, Indians! Go, Indians!"

We are winning! We are winning! Hey, it's my turn finally. I am up now to bat. The coach pitches the ball, and I duck. He pitches again, and I move out of the batter's box.

My dad comes up to me and says, "Anthony, you'd better hit the ball, or I'll take you out."

I'm thinking, *Why is he not working with me?* I'm getting ready. It takes a few pitches before I really hit the grand slam. I think it's time for me to hit the ball. The coach pitches the ball, and I hit it.

My mom starts yelling, "Run, Anthony! Run!"

And I start to run fast. I run so fast that I slide to first base, and the umpire yells, "Safe!"

Aha! I made it! I made it! And that's all, folks. No more running. Since I have made it to first base and I am the last to bat, the coaches want me to run to second and third base and finally home. The score is six up, and the other team is up.

It's the final inning, and they haven't scored any runs as of yet. I guess this is going to be a tied game. My dad always says we are all winners, no matter what.

I say, "Yeah, right. Is that what you think?"

Well, it's okay because next year I am not playing baseball. I'm going to play flag football. I am glad the season is over. It does end with a tied game.

Now here comes my mom. I wonder why she's coming on the field. She goes to each of the coaches and gives them a gift for all their hard work and dedication to us. Boy, they didn't do much but yell, scream, and throw the ball to us. Oh, don't forget they also hit us with the ball. Besides, I don't think they had any hard work being coaches. My dad had to do all the work half of the time, and the other dads … well, let me tell you … if you thought my dad were lazy, you should have seen these dads.

I am glad it's over though because I am going to New York City to see my grandma Gladys. Oh yeah! Oh yeah! Whoopee, no more baseball! Yeah! We all had so much fun playing. Let me tell you that I think my dad did a very good job coaching, but don't tell him I said that. I don't want him to think that he is the bomb! Who knows? Maybe I'll play next year. I have to think about it really hard before I say anything to my dad.

I'm so proud of my dad, and when my mom gives my dad the picture frame, he is happy. Yes, she got a frame with a team picture custom made for him. The frame reads, "Thank you for all your hard work and dedication."

Well, that's my dad! He smiles. You know he is excited and happy that he starts blushing too. I've never seen my dad blush. Hey, that's our secret, okay? Honestly after receiving all the gifts from the parents, my dad looks like he wants to cry too. But don't say anything.

You know what's so funny? And I know they will get mad at me, but I think Eric got the crying from my dad. The picture frame is engraved with our team name and the year. It says "Indians 2004." That's my team. Every dad who helped coach gets a frame for doing a good job with the kids.

I'm confused. What do they mean "with the kids"? All they did was tell us to do stretches, warm up, run two laps around the field, catch, do jumping jacks and head-shoulders-knees-toes, move side to side, and everything you can imagine. And you say, "Good job"?

No, you're wrong. They did a great job, even though they made us do all the hard work. This is only Minor B Little League Baseball.

Kristopher's Game

After the season is over, we have no other choice but to go watch Kris play his game. His team has made it to the playoffs. I am so excited for Kris. He is good, especially because he uses my dad's baseball glove. We call it "the lucky glove" because it's been my dad's since he was thirteen years old. He is old now, and he can't use it for softball.

Oh man! Did I tell you? My dad wasn't only a first-time coach during the season. He also umpires some of the games, and he does that really well. He is working Kris's game today, and he is getting ready.

My mom is at the snack bar today. My mom hates doing the snack bar because she can't cheer from there. Since she's doing the snack bar and my dad is umpiring the game, I get to go back and forth to update Mom on the game. And she can also buy me sunflower seeds, Big League gum, and a yellow PowerAde. Kris always gets a Red PowerAde with Big League gum. Eric, if you let him choose what he wants, will order the whole snack bar.

Here we go. The game is starting, and my dad is calling for a batter. Man! He is always yelling for something.

"Batter up, Coach! We need a batter up!"

Here comes the first batter from Kris's team since the other team already struck out. As the kid from Kris's team is walking toward the batter box, he practices his swings. He steps in the batter's box and is ready. The pitcher winds up and releases the ball.

My dad yells, "Ball one!"

He pitches again.

My dad yells, "Strike one!"

And then the pitcher pitches again. Oh boy! It hits the batter.

My dad yells, "Take your base!"

This looks like it's going to be an exciting game, but to me, it's not going to be as thrilling as my game since I had the best game of the season with my dad being my coach.

Here comes the next batter, and that's Kris. Go, Kristopher!

There goes my mom yelling, "Go, Yankees! Go, Kris! You can do this, baby."

The pitcher winds up and pitches.

Kris swings.

My dad yells, "Strike one!"

My mom yells, "Kris, you know how to get that ball! It's all yours."

Like she really knows what she is taking about—right, I think.

The pitcher throws again.

And my dad yells, "Ball one!"

Everyone is clapping and yelling, "Go, Yankees!"

The pitcher winds up and throws again.

And my dad yells, "Ball two!"

And the guy on first base steals second. Go! Go! Go! Yeah!

The second base umpire yells, "Safe!"

And everyone jumps up from the seats. I wonder, *Why didn't they do that for my game? All they did was clap. That's it!*

So, the coach from the other team walks up to the pitcher's mound. He talks to the player, and all of a sudden, here comes another pitcher to replace the first one. The new pitcher winds up, and he throws.

All you hear is, "Strike two!"

My mom yells out, "We need a new ump." And then she smiles.

Kris is ready, and here comes another pitch. He swings that bat as if he were playing his violin.

My dad yells, "Foul ball!"

Oh, there the pitcher releases the right pitch! Kris swings and hits the ball. And yes! He gets to run to first base.

The first base coach yells, "Safe!"

My mom is jumping up and yelling, "You go, Kris!" and "You're the man! Kris, you're a beast!"

Oh yeah! Now he's called the Kris the Beast at every game. He's like that famous baseball player from Puerto Rico, Roberto Clemente. Mom always tells Kris that if he continues playing baseball, he is going to make it like these famous people did. My mom actually tells this to all of us, but she also tells us that school is first above all things. We need an education in order to become famous. Yeah! I tell her I am already famous in school.

Gee! All this talking, and I forgot to tell you that the next batter after Kris gets out, and the next kid is walked. The bases are now loaded. This is an exciting game.

This game has been so exciting that the score is tied by the last inning. Oh man! Are we ever going to go home? I am bored, tired, and hungry. I want to go home already! The game is over.

Kristopher's team wins by one run. Yes! It's over! Finally!

CPSIA information can be obtained
at www.ICGtesting.com
Printed in the USA
LVOW05s2313180717
541845LV00045B/1185/P